Bing Crosby and Bob Hope: The Golden Era of Hollywood's Most Popular Show Business Stars

By Charles River Editors

Bing Crosby

About Charles River Editors

Charles River Editors was founded by Harvard and MIT alumni to provide superior editing and original writing services, with the expertise to create digital content for publishers across a vast range of subject matter. In addition to providing original digital content for third party publishers, Charles River Editors republishes civilization's greatest literary works, bringing them to a new generation via ebooks.

Introduction

Crosby in the trailer for *Road to Singapore*

Bing Crosby (1903-1977)

"I think popular music in this country is one of the few things in the twentieth century that have made giant strides in reverse." – Bing Crosby

In 1948, American polls rated Bing Crosby "the most admired man alive", and it's no surprise given how popular he was across every major form of entertainment during the decade. With a string of major hits, Crosby was the most popular singer in the country during that era, with classic songs like "White Christmas" helping pave the way for other singers as varied as Bob Hope, Dean Martin, and Frank Sinatra. In fact, young Sinatra modeled his clothing and style after Crosby, who was his idol growing up. And as good as he was at singing, Crosby's work with radio technology helped pave the way for multitracking songs and making it possible to broadcast the same radio programs across the country without cutting another live version. All told, Crosby sold an estimated 500 million records in the 20th century.

In addition to being one of America's most beloved singers and an accomplished radio presence, Crosby not only made popular movies but acted well enough to be critically acclaimed. His *Road To…* movie series with Bob Hope produced some of the best-selling movies of the 1940s, 1950s, and 1960s, and he won an Oscar for Best Actor in *Going My Way* (1944) by playing Father Chuck O'Malley. When he was nominated for the same role in the 1945 sequel *The Bells of St. Mary's*, he became one of just 4 people nominated for two Oscars for playing the same role.

Bing Crosby and Bob Hope examines the life and career of one of America's greatest and most versatile entertainers. Along with pictures of important people, places, and events, you will learn about Kelly like never before.

Bob Hope in 1986. Picture taken by Allan Warren

Bob Hope (1903-2003)

"You never get tired unless you stop and take time for it." – Bob Hope

Of all the show business icons in American history, one of the most beloved was Bob Hope, whose career spanned over 6 decades across film, television, vaudeville, comedy, and touring and earned him too many accolades to count. On the day of his 100th birthday, more than half of the states in America declared it "Bob Hope Day", a sign of just how monumental and influential he was as an entertainer. Along the way, he performed so many United Service Organization (USO) tours visiting troops that Congress made him the "first and only honorary veteran of the U.S. armed forces." Incredibly, he was given honorary awards for his career at the Academy Awards nearly 40 years before his death, and decades before he actually retired from public life. By the time he reached his twilight, he was an instantly recognized institution unto himself.

All of that would have been impressive for any American, let alone someone who was actually born in England with the name Leslie Townes Hope. Indeed, the quintessential American entertainer wouldn't actually move to the country until he was 4, and while his English roots may have helped his impressive impersonation of Charlie Chaplin when Hope was merely a teen, he quickly became an American through and through. He later claimed he changed his first name to Bob because it had a folksy feel to it, and he definitely gave off that kind of aura throughout his 5 decades doing USO tours, his 4 decades making films, his television career of . In addition to his versatile career that ranged from Broadway to comedy, he was an accomplished athlete who once quipped that all of the money he made went towards his greens fees. In fact, Hope became notorious for carrying a golf club around, so much so that Stephen Colbert paid homage to him by carrying a golf club during his own USO performances in 2009.

Bing Crosby and Bob Hope examines the life and career of one of America's greatest entertainers, tracing his rise to stardom and the towering legacy he left behind. Along with pictures of important people, places, and events, you will learn about Bob Hope like never before.

Chapter 1: Little Bing

"Honestly, I think I've stretched a talent which is so thin it's almost transparent over a quite unbelievable term of years." – Bing Crosby

"Everyone knows I'm just a big, good-natured slob." – Bing Crosby

Harry Lillis Crosby, Jr. was born on May 3, 1903 in Tacoma, Washington to parents Harry Lillis, Sr. and Catherine, who were devout Catholics and members of America's burgeoning middle class. Harry was a bookkeeper and an indirect descendant of Puritan forefather William Brewster, while Catherine was a second generation American, her grandparents having emigrated from Ireland in the previous century. Bing would take after his father but end up being his mother's son, as his own father would later note: "My wife really knows more about him than I do. Not that he is a stranger to me! But mother – well, you know how boys always act toward their mothers. I guess I've always been the easy-going father. Bing takes after me in that respect. Nobody can rush him either. I remember the times I'd come home from work and how often I'd be greeted with the story of some disturbing antic of his during the day. My wife always would say, 'Now, Harry, you must speak to Bing. He's been very hard to manage today.' I'd look very indignant, promise some sort of punishment, then watch Kate do the disciplining. I just couldn't bring myself to punish Bing – or any of the boys."

In addition to being a bookkeeper, Harry was also an amateur carpenter who built the house on North J Street in which Harry Jr., his fourth son, was born. The next two children, both girls, were born in a home the family rented when they moved to Spokane in 1906, but by the time the seventh (and last) baby was born, the family would be living in a new and larger home Harry built on Sharp Avenue in that city. It was shortly after they moved into the new home that Harry, Jr. received his now famous nickname. The local paper ran a comedy feature each Sunday called "The Bingville Bugle", a humorous piece that purported to be a sort of redneck newsletter. It featured "local gossip" and poorly spelled articles, as well as "advertisements" for imaginary products. Little Harry loved the articles and often persuaded a neighbor, 15 year old Valentine Hobart, to read them to him. Hobart in turn began to call the little boy "Bingo from Bingville", which eventually evolved into the legendary nickname Bing.

From the beginning, the Crosby's were a musical family, with a piano in the parlor and chances for the children to perform little numbers when company came over. However, as Bing got older, he began to want something more than just ordinary family music making, and in this, he was encouraged in his ambitions by his uncle: "My mother had a brother, George Harrigan, a great singer in the Tacoma – Seattle area. ...of course his theme song was 'Harrigan,' taken from the Cohen song. And he was the biggest favorite singing around that area that ever occurred there. He was a great guy and had a terrific voice – big, high, loud, powerful tenor. Any time he appeared, everybody'd holler, 'Harrigan,' and he'd go: 'H – A – double R – I – G – A – N spells Harrigan/Devil a man could say a word against me,' and I learned a lot just watching him. He could tell stories in any dialect you ever heard of. He should have gone into show business.... He'd have been a sensational star with his ability to do dialect stories and sing."

Unfortunately, all the good cheer in the world couldn't prevent the Crosby family from falling on hard times during the years leading up to America's entry into World War I. The city of Spokane outlawed the sale of liquor, so Harry was laid off for a time from the local brewery, and while her husband looked for work, Kate focused her attention on children's futures. She was particularly optimistic about Bing, who she believed had inherited much of her brother's singing ability, and she began to encourage him to sing at local church and civic functions. While his acts were well-received, and he enjoyed the spotlight like any young kid, Bing initially had mixed feelings about performing publicly, as he later explained: "My mother dressed me up in some fantastic attire, the knickerbockers and the flowing ties. That embarrassed me more than the singing, I believe. And of course the fellas I ran around with all thought that singing was for girls or sissies, certainly not for anyone who was going to be an athlete. Because we were mostly, as a group, concerned with rock fights and going down to the mill pond and running the logs and hooking rides on railroad trains and robbing the bakery wagon and things of that caliber, which were considered a little more adventurous and colorful than standing up in front of the ladies' sodality and singing 'One Fleeting Hour.'"

Given how devout Bing's family was, it's no surprise that his parents were determined to make sure all of the children received a solid Catholic education, no matter the expense or how tight money was. Thus, when the time came for Bing to enter high school, he joined his brothers at Gonzaga High School, located on the campus of the Jesuit run Gonzaga University. For the Crosby boys, the location could not have been any better, because the campus bordered their home on Sharp Avenue. In fact, that house was later absorbed into the University campus, and for a time it even served as the headquarters for the university's alumni association.

Not surprisingly, Bing's background with the Jesuits would become a topic of conversation in later years after he played the famous Father O'Malley in *Going My Way* and *The Bells of St. Mary's*. While much has been said, good and bad, about the Catholic educational system, for his part Bing only had praise for his alma mater. In one radio interview during the 1950s, he shared with his listeners the impact his high school and college years made on his life: "The university was only 25 or 35 years old then and there were still some of the pioneer staff of the Jesuit order, then around 75 or 80 years of age, who had come out there with the Indian missions, as Father Cataldo and some of his followers had done, and they were brilliant men, men with great backgrounds in the missionary field, and I was much impressed with them, of course, because they had many stories to tell, incidents that happened in the first settlement, working with the Indians, and I was much impressed with their piety."

Naturally, Bing was interested in many extracurricular activities while in school, including singing, comedy, and also acting in Gonzaga's theatrical group. Despite being known for comedy, he often played more serious roles, such as Antony in Shakespeare's *Julius Caesar*. He also played baseball and swam during the summer months, as well as working for the school newspaper. Overall, he was a solid all-around student whose only vice seems to have been being something of a class clown, and when he graduated in 1920, he seemed destined for the kind of semi-prosperous life in Spokane or some similarly middle class town that his own family had.

As it turned out, the seeds for Bing's future stardom, planted by his mother, had already been nourished by a very different source. When he was 14 years old, Bing got his first significant job working as a property boy for the Spokane Auditorium, a local house that hosted some of the biggest names in vaudeville during that era. Given his job, Bing got to see them all, and one of his favorites was Al Jolson, who fascinated the teenager with his off the cuff ad libbing and spoofs of popular songs.

Jolson

In spite of his growing love for entertainment, Bing still didn't consider it a valid career path when he entered Gonzaga University in the fall of 1920, but even though his mother hoped he would study for the priesthood, the young man, though devout, knew that wasn't his calling either. To soften Kate's disappointment, he agreed to study law, a profession considered equally respectable to her, and Bing also played baseball and studied hard, becoming popular with both his peers and professors.

Bing's student photo at Gonzaga

However, as his college years wore on, Crosby found himself drawn more and more to the stage, beginning with acting in student productions during his freshmen year and expanding his involvement as he went along. One form of entertainment that he thoroughly enjoyed was the minstrel show, which are racially offensive to modern viewers but were productions that went back decades and had evolved through the years to be more about characters than about race. In fact, they were so customary during the early 20th century that even such a staid college as Gonzaga allowed it. Later in his career, Crosby would resurrect some of the characters he played in college in some of his films.

In 1923, Crosby was approached by some high school students with a favor; they were forming a new band and need someone older and more experienced to help them get started. Always close to his younger siblings, Bing took pity on them and agreed to join the group they called the Musicaladers. For the next two years, the band performed locally at high-school dances and parties, but as the boys grew up, it became harder to get everyone together to practice, so the group disbanded in 1925. But by that point, Crosby had graduated from college and was ready to pursue music more seriously, so he teamed up with Al Rinker to form a singing duet. Through Rinker's sister, Mildred Bailey, they met the famous bandleader Paul Whiteman, whose orchestra was the most popular musical act in the country during the 1920s. Whiteman liked the young men and their sound, so he hired them to play at the Tivoli Theatre in Chicago.

Mildred Bailey

Crosby and Rinker

Thus, the two packed their bags and moved across country to the Windy City, dreaming of fame and fortune, and when they premiered at the Tivoli on December 6, 1926, they were working for what was to them the grand sum of $150 per week. Rinker later recalled their premier: "[Whiteman] told the audience that he had heard two young boys singing an ice cream parlor in a little town out West, called Walla Walla. 'They sang some songs and I wondered what they were doing in Walla Walla. These kids are too good, too good for Walla Walla, so I asked them to join my band. This is their first appearance with the band and here they are. I want you to meet Crosby and Rinker. Come on out boys.' The little piano was moved onstage and Bing and I came out from the wings. All I know is that we got a big hand after our first song and even more applause on our second number. To top it all, we were called back for an encore. That was our first appearance on the big time. You can bet we were too happy guys. Whiteman came over to us after the show and said, 'Well, how do you feel? I knew they'd like you. Welcome to the band!'"

Whiteman

Their work at the Tivoli opened the doors for them to make their first album, a very poor recording of "I've Got the Girl." Accompanied by Don Clark's Orchestra, the two sounded pretty odd on the single issued by Columbia Records; the album had been recorded at a slower speed than planned, making the two sound somewhat like Alvin and the Chipmunks when it was played at full 78 rpm speed. Thankfully, their live work was impressive enough that Whiteman hired a third man, Harry Barris, who was not only an excellent pianist but also aspired to be a songwriter. Performing together, the three became known as "The Rhythm Boys", and they toured the country with Whteman's troupe, which allowed them to perform with some of the best musicians in the business, including Tommy and Jimmy Dorsey and Hoagy Carmichael.

While the men all performed and made records together and in variously arranged smaller groups, it soon became obvious that Crosby was the best of the group. In 1928, he released his first chart topping single, a gentle, crooning version of "Ol' Man River." Two years later, The Rhythm Boys appeared in their first picture, *King of Jazz*, which was billed as "100% talkie," a boast sure to catch the public's attention. Though they did not have speaking roles, they were featured in several musical numbers and their voices translated well to film, ensuring they also appeared in a short subject later that year. This film proved to be significant to Crosby's career because it was the first picture in which he was given billing, although he couldn't help but wonder about what would've happened had he sang one of the film's numbers instead of John Boles: "I have often wondered what might have happened to me if I had sung 'The Song of the Dawn'. It certainly helped Boles - on the strength of it, he got a lot of pictures. I must say, he had a bigger voice and a better delivery for that kind of song than I had. My crooning style wouldn't have been good for such a number, which was supposed to have been delivered a la breve, like 'The Vagabond Song'. I might have flopped with it. I might have been cut out of 'The King of Jazz'. I might never have been given another crack at a song in any picture." *King of Jazz* did well enough that Crosby went on to appear as himself in *Reaching for the Moon* in 1930.

Chapter 2: The Vaudeville Boy

"I left England when I was four because I found out I could never be king." – Bob Hope

"I was born in 1903 at Eltham in England. Eltham is about ten miles from Charring Cross Station. It's pronounced without the h. When I was about two years old, my father and mother moved to Bristol. My mother was the daughter of a Welsh sea captain. Her name was Avis Townes. My dad's name was William Henry Hope." – Bob Hope

Poor Avis Townes. She had given up her career as an opera singer to marry William Hope, a stonemason, in 1891, but when she had a healthy baby boy, she was happy. A firstborn son was surely what every man wanted, and when her second son was born, she probably thought it was nice since the boys could be playmates. The third boy meant that she wouldn't have to buy any new baby clothes, even though she wanted a girl. Her fourth son came next, and when she found out she was pregnant, she figured she would have a girl this time.

As it turned out, she did not. On May 29, 1903, Avis gave birth to her fifth son, choosing the slightly feminine sounding name of Leslie for the boy and then giving him her own maiden name, Townes, for a middle name. Traditionally, this honor would have been reserved for her first daughter, but she was tired of waiting, and this proved to be a wise move, since the future Bob Hope would go on to have two more younger siblings, both boys. Hope later joked, "I grew up with six brothers. That's how I learned to dance - waiting for the bathroom."

Bob Hope as a kid

Although he was born in England, the Hope family came to the United States in 1908 and settled in Cleveland, Ohio. The following year, Leslie started school and quickly found that both his accent and his name were sources of humor for his classmates: "My first day in school in Cleveland the other kids asked me, 'What's your name?' When I said 'Les Hope,' they switched it to Hopeless. It got to be quite a rib and caused some scuffling and a few bloody ski-snoots for me."

Those weren't the young boy's only problems. Money was tight in the Hope home, which was exacerbated by the fact William often drank too much and had trouble finding work. This all but forced Avis to be the backbone of the family, and in addition to raising her seven sons, she also took in boarders to help make ends meet. As a result, the boys were expected to contribute financially as soon as they were old enough to get jobs. For his part, Les began by selling papers, but he soon moved on to street performing, which included dancing, singing, and performing comedy routines on streetcars around Cleveland. People would throw him coins that he would carry home to his mother, but just as important was the pride he got when he received positive reactions for his performances. As a teenager, Les decided to enter some of the talent contests that were popular in early 20th century America, and using the name Lester Hope, he won his first contest in 1915 for his impersonation of Charlie Chaplin.

Hope as a teen

Under pressure from his family, Hope continued to try to find a more traditional kind of steady work, but his heart was never in it. When his brother Fred hired him as a meat cutter in his butcher shop, Les didn't cut meat or wait on customers but instead spent his time singing and dancing around the shop and doing little comedy routines for the bemused patrons who came in. While the public enjoyed his hijincks, Fred did not.

Not all of Hope's performances were friendly, however. With a name like Leslie Hope, the future Bob Hope learned to fight in the schoolyard and on the streets. In fact, for a short time, he even tried his hand at boxing, and even though he won three of the four official bouts he fought in the late 1910s, he ultimately decided that the ring was no place for him. Of course, that didn't stop him from later joking about his short lived boxing career: "I was very popular because I had a peculiar weaving, bobbing style the crowd loved to watch. I used to weave and bob around the ring for ten minutes after the other guy had won and gone home. I'll never forget my first fight. When the bell rang I danced to the center of the ring – then they carried me to the corner. Then the bell rang again and I danced to the center of the ring – then they carried me to my corner."

Of course, singing and dancing weren't the only things on young Les' mind. He also had a girlfriend, Mildred Rosequist, with whom he was quite smitten. Like him, she had performing aspirations, but even though she consistently refused his romantic proposals that they get married on her lunch breaks, she did agree to become his dancing partner. The two took lessons together and subsequently landed a short, three-day gig dancing at a local nightclub. Their act proved to be pretty popular, and Hope now believed he had found his true calling.

Bob and Mildred

However, Mildred wasn't as serious about a career on stage, so Hope dropped her as a stage partner and teamed up with Lloyd Durbin instead. The two men worked well together and were soon playing regularly at local clubs and dives. It was at one of these performances that Hope got his big break; in 1925, silent film comedian Fatty Arbuckle attended one of their performances and liked what he saw, so he offered the two men work with a touring company called Hurley's Jolly Follies. When Durbin died suddenly of food poisoning while on the road, a despondent Hope formed the Dancemedians. Hope's new partner was a man named George Byrne, and according to him, "George was pink-cheeked and naive. He looked like a choir boy. He was real quiet. Real Ohio. He was a smooth dancer and had a likable personality. We became good friends. And later on, his sister married my brother George."

Arbuckle

A lot of the recurring themes and acts in vaudeville featured performances that 21st century audiences would find morally and culturally offensive, and the Dancemedians were one such performance. For example, Hope and Byrne created a dance and comedy routine featuring a pair of conjoined twins called the Hilton Sisters, and as he would later remember, "Then we got a job dancing with Daisy and Violet Hilton, the Siamese twins. At first it was a funny sensation to dance with the Siamese twins. They danced back to back, but they were wonderful girls and it got to the very enjoyable in an unusual sort of way." The sisters tap-danced with Hope and Byrne, who also appeared on stage as conjoined siblings.

While that aspect of the routine was certainly insensitive, a more disturbing part of the performance is that the two men often performed in blackface. But in its own day, the act was popular and received good reviews, including the following: "But for the premier honors of the entire bill, Hope and Byrne came through with flying colors in the eccentric dance. Friends, it was a knockout. There has never been anything better in this house of this kind. They easily take first place without contest. They tore the house down, came back for more and got it."

Hope would later be questioned about his decision to play what is now considered such an offensive act, and he tried to explain to the modern audience what made the minstrel shows acceptable at that time: "People thought they were making fun of blacks, but it was just a way of playing characters, you know? Minstrel shows were very large. At one theater where I was playing and getting very little money, I got to the theater late and I didn't have time to put the black on and so I walked out with my regular face. After the show, the theater manager came back and said, 'Don't put that stuff on your face. You got a face that saves jokes.' In those days, you did blackface but you downplayed the minstrel aspect."

He took the manager's advice, but he also worked to add more comedy to the act, and he later described another act: "We wore high hats and spats and carried a cane for this. Then we made quick changes to firemen's outfits and danced real fast to 'If You Knew Susie,' at a rapid ta–da–da–da–dah tempo, while the drummer rang a fire bell. At the end of the routine I squirted water from a concealed bulb at the brass section of the orchestra in the pit. It not only made an attractive finish but it had the advantage of drowning a few musicians."

In the summer of 1927, Hope and Byrnes were chosen for a very small part in the musical *Sidewalks of New York*, and the popular musical's success introduced Hope to the more sophisticated world of Broadway. Unfortunately, as the show ran on, the director decided he was no longer in need of their services and let them go. When they returned to vaudeville, they decided to emphasize the acting and comedic aspect of their act over the singing and dancing, but this proved to be less popular with their audiences than they had hoped, and they soon found themselves again without work.

Next, the two got a small job in Pennsylvania, and while there, the manager of the theater asked Hope to come on stage at the end of the evening and announce the next week's act. Hope did so, but in his own unique way, cracking jokes about the next performer. The audience ate this up, and someone encouraged Hope to give up singing and dancing altogether and make comedy his career. After talking things over with Bryne, the two men agreed that Hope should try going out on his own. He later recalled, "I went out, bought a big red bow tie, white cotton gloves…a cigar and a small bowler which jiggled up and down when I bounced onstage. I'd picked up some new material here and there, plus a few things I'd though up. For an encore I did a song and dance. I scored well even if I was scoring in a Lilliputian world." Like some of his previous acts, Hope appeared in blackface during part of his first solo act.

While trying to launch his solo career, Hope lived at home and played small clubs around Cleveland. After some limited success, he dropped the blackface but kept the bowler hat and moved to Chicago, then the vaudeville capital of the country. After weeks of failure and near starvation, he finally landed a job as emcee for the West Englewood Theatre, and in turn that led to a job at the Stratford, one of the nicer vaudeville houses in Chicago. Hope would later reflect that it was at the Stratford that he really began to perfect his craft: "One of the things I learned at the Stratford Theater was to have enough courage to wait. I'd stand there waiting for them to get it for a long time. Longer than any other comedian had the guts to wait. My idea was to let them know who was running things."

From Stratford, Hope went on a tour of a number of houses throughout the Midwest, and it was also around this time that he decided to change his first name to Bob. He felt it had a friendlier, more "common man" feel than Les, or as he described it, a "Hiya, fellas!" kind of name. This proved to be important for his work in Texas, where he initially had a problem relating to the hard-bitten people of the Southwest.

Chapter 3: Fits and Starts in Show Business

"Well we are winging our way westward to have a truly marvelous time of it. ... Not only are we having a great time but my name is being prominently featured in newspapers and in broadcasts and considerable invaluable publicity that redounds to me. What awaits us on the coast is as yet problematical and whether we get much of a break in the picture or not I can't tell. However, I intend to bear down heavily and really try to accomplish something worthwhile." - Bing Crosby in a letter to his mother in 1930.

"I have seen what a laugh can do. It can transform almost unbearable tears into something bearable, even hopeful." – Bob Hope

As the calendar turned over to the new decade, Crosby made two major changes in his personal life. The first may seem trivial to some but never was to him. While filming *The King of Jazz*, Crosby decided to join some of the other members of the cast in a game of golf, and even though he had never played before, he had worked as a caddie when he was 12 and had picked up some skills then. Through the years, golf would become Crosby's favorite sport, while also doubling as his primary source of physical exercise. Though he joked that his golfing was "woeful but I will never surrender", Crosby would later compete in both the British and the United States Amateur Championships with a two handicap. He was also the champion of the Lake Golf Club in Hollywood on five separate occasions and even made a hole in one on the 16th hole of the Cypress Point Club.

Similarly, right around the same time, Hope took up golfing as well, and he later described his introduction to golf: "I had tried to play in Cleveland during the 1920s, but I just had no feel for the game. I had never taken lessons and I was terrible but during the spring of 1930 on the Orpheum circuit I'd been waiting around the hotel lobby in the late morning when the Diamond Brothers, another act, would come down with their golf clubs. They played every day. One day I said, 'Oh, hell, I'll go out there with you.' I hit a bag of practice balls and played a few holes. It was fun." For the rest of his life, golf would also be an integral part of Hope's career. He often carried a golf club on stage when doing a monologue, and he worked golf humor into many of his acts, including one in which he remarked, "It's wonderful how you can start out with three strangers in the morning, play 18 holes, and by the time the day is over you have three solid enemies." In 1978, he even putted on stage against a two year old named Tiger Woods.

Hope putting in President Nixon's office in March 1973

The second change that Crosby made to his personal life was in giving up his wild bachelor life to settle down. He began dating 17 year old Dixie Lee, a rising singer in her own right. Like most young men his age, Crosby had dated a number of women through the years, but this one was different, as he wrote home to his mother, "Incidentally I met a girl the other night whom I think you'd like. Her name is Dixie Lee and she works for Fox. Been taking her out quite a bit lately, and she's kind of got me thinking. Don't get alarmed though, nothing serious yet. Or maybe there is." Not only was there something serious about their relationship, but there was also something important that Crosby did not to share with his Catholic mother: Lee was

Protestant.

In spite of that crucial difference, the two married on September 29, 1930. By this time, Crosby felt his career was secure enough to support a wife, and Dixie felt that Bing had his drinking under control. Though she was never much of a drinker herself, Dixie began to drink socially in order to keep her husband company, which would sadly lead to her own problems with the bottle later in life.

Dixie Lee

But all that was in the future, and for the time being, they were two young newlyweds in love. At first, it seemed that Lee might join her husband in a film career. She already had several movies to her credit and continued to make more during the early years of their marriage, but the birth of their first child Gary brought those plans to an end in 1933. Though she did return to the movies briefly in early 1934, her career ended for good with the birth of twins Dennis and Phillip later that year. The family was rounded out by son Lindsey in 1938.

Crosby's sons. From L-R: Gary, Lindsey, Phillip and Dennis below

While his family was growing, so was Crosby's career. He released his first solo album in September 1931, and within a few months, he signed a contract to record for Brunswick Records. He was also given his own radio show by CBS, during which he would come on the air once a week and sing for 15 minutes. The public came to love his music, and several more of his songs made it to the top of the charts by the end of the year, including the memorably titled "I Found a Million Dollar Baby (in a Five and Ten Cent Store)." In fact, Crosby was somehow involved with 10 of the top 50 songs of 1931.

One of the major driving forces behind his popularity is that Crosby brought a new style of singing to music. Up until the 1930s, most performers had gotten their starts and been shaped by their days on stage, so they were accustomed to singing loudly and with force in order for their voices to be heard and appreciated even by listeners in the "cheap seats." Bob Hope later recalled how difficult it was to adjust to singing softly into a microphone so as not to blow out the eardrums of the sound technician. Crosby, on the other hand, didn't have this problem; though he had done some stage work, it was generally in front of smaller, more intimate audiences. As a result, his style was naturally softer and gentler, giving him the ability to make listeners feel like he was singing directly to them about life and love. Henry Pleasants, the author of *The Great American Popular Singers*, described it as "singing in American", while the people who first heard Crosby sing called it crooning. From the beginning, Crosby was "the king of the crooners."

   Part of the credit for Crosby's style also goes to Jack Kapp, who managed him for both Brunswick and Decca records. He often reminded Crosby that his radio audience could not see him, so there was no need to put his efforts into the hand motions he had used as a jazz musician. Instead, he encouraged Crosby to sing from deep in his soul and put his emotional background into it. Al Jolson also deserves some of the credit for shaping Crosby's career, because it was from Jolson that Crosby learned to use careful phrasing to make a song's lyrics sound relatable to his audience. Crosby in turn became the inspiration for others, as band leader Tommy Dorsey later explained, "I used to tell Sinatra over and over, there's only one singer you ought to listen to and his name is Crosby. All that matters to him is the words, and that's the only thing that ought to for you, too."

Crosby and Jack Kapp

At first, the public and critics were not sure Crosby had staying power. Some said he was just a flash in the pan, while others referred to his edging out competitor Russ Columbo in the "Battle of the Baritones." However, as time went on, it became apparent that Crosby was on top to stay. At that time, the early 1930s came to be known as the time when "Bing Was King."

Meanwhile, Hope had begun to think that the vaudeville stage was not big enough for his talents, and as he clamored for more attention and bigger audiences, this inevitably compelled him to go West and try to break into the burgeoning motion picture industry. While that decision would obviously work out, it initially seemed like a mistake when he bombed his screen test for Pathe Pictures in Culver City, California. He later described his first experience seeing himself on screen: "I thought it was strange that nobody else was there until I looked around and saw that even the projectionists were wearing gas masks. My nose hit the screen 10 minutes before the rest of me. I always knew my body had angles but didn't realize how much they stuck out. It was awful. I felt I was watching a stranger. I didn't want to know. Of course there was no audience and no laughter, but even so I couldn't believe how bad I was. When the lights came up I wanted to get out fast."

Gathering what was left of his pride around him, he returned to vaudeville and the Orpheum circuit, but motion pictures continued to haunt him. He would frequently come on to do his comedy routine immediately after the climactic ending of a dramatic feature, and no matter how he tried, he faced increasing challenges in getting the audience to accept one man standing alone on the stage when they had just seen several projected across the screen.

Nonetheless, the high point of his stage career came in the early spring of 1931, when he was booked to play the New York Palace, and in 1932, Hope returned to Broadway as the emcee for *Ballyhoo in 1932*. Though the show only ran for 12 weeks, it gave Hope a chance to improvise and improve his comedic timing. He also had several opportunities to make guest appearances on local radio shows, which proved to be a bigger challenge than he initially anticipated. He later remembered, "It all seemed so strange, talking into a microphone instead of playing in front of a real audience. I was nervous on the first radio shows and the engineers couldn't figure out why they heard a thumping noise when I did my routines until they found out I was kicking the mike after each joke." Hope also began working with a man who would help shape his career when he and Bing Crosby appeared together for the first time at the Capital Theater.

During this time, Hope often performed with a young woman named Grace Louise Troxell, and their excellent timing both on and off stage soon bloomed into a romance. After several years of performing together across the country, the two eloped in January 1933, but Hope had never wanted to marry her in the first place and had only done so out of a sense of rewarding her loyalty to him through the years. The marriage only lasted a few months before the two agreed to divorce and go their separate ways.

By this time, Hope knew that the days of vaudeville and live comedy were coming to an end, and while people would willingly pay their nickels and dimes to see someone perform in a movie, they were not so inclined to buy tickets to listen to someone tell jokes. Moreover, they could just as easily listen to that at home on their radios. Even still, Hope returned to the Palace and continued to perform there until he was offered a part in another Broadway show. This time his role was much larger; he played the lead as Huckleberry Haines in the popular musical *Roberta*. However, Hope did not enjoy either the musical or his part in it. For one thing, it was supposed to be a comedy but was too melodramatic to lend itself easily to humor, and when he tried to come up with gags and one-liners that would liven things up, most of his ideas were either rejected or fell flat. The critics were not impressed either, as one solemnly intoned, "The humors of *Roberta* are no great shakes and are smugly declaimed by Bob Hope, who insists on being the life of the party and actually would be more amusing if he were Fred Allen."

At the same time, Hope's time with *Roberta* was not a complete waste, because he met Dolores Reade, a singer at one of the clubs the cast often visited after the show. According to Bob, it was a passionate, whirlwind romance: "From then on I was at the Vogue every night, waiting to take Dolores home. I must have given the doorman at her apartment hundreds of dollars in tips to let me park in front of the joint and sit there with her…. It was our Inspiration Point, our Flirtation Walk…there in front of the Delmonico on Ninth Avenue." In order to spend as much time as possible with his new love, Hope invited Dolores to join his act in the spring of 1934. The two became engaged that August and married in November, the beginning of what would end up being a 69 year marriage. In between, Hope starred in *Say When* on Broadway, a comedy about two radio men who fall in love with debutante sisters. It was a hit, but production problems forced it to close before the end of the year.

Bob and Dolores Hope

Chapter 4: On the Big Screen and Over the Air

"If I'm going to get by in pictures, it's going to be as a singer, with about as much acting as you would expect from a guy standing in front of a microphone." – Bing Crosby

"Once or twice I've been described as a light comedian. I consider this the most accurate description of my abilities I've ever seen." – Bing Crosby

Ironically, Crosby would be known as the radio pioneer, but it was Hope whose radio career first began in earnest. By 1935, Hope was looking for something new. He was ready to settle down into married life and did not want to continue to keep the hectic schedule that stage acting demanded, so he jumped at the chance for the emcee position on the popular radio show *Intimate Review*. Unlike his previous radio work, *Intimate Review* was done before a live audience, and their laughter gave Hope the instant feedback he was used to, which also made it easier for him to time his material. Still, he had trouble remembering that his primary audience could not see him and could only respond to what he said and how he said it. One review observed, "Hope is intermittently very funny. At other times either his material falters or his deliver is a bit too lackadaisical. In general Hope should avoid too much nonchalance. It's a luxury not allowed by radio. He must work to put himself and his stuff over, as the poker face mugging that means something on the rostrum doesn't percolate through the cosmos. Hope is easy to take but hard to remember. His problem then is one of emphasis. A good central idea rather than reliance on kidding the announcer and the patter of the bright persiflage would hold more weight."

As Hope continued to refine his radio persona, he decided to add a female partner to play off of; in the past, he had great success working with Louise, and most of the other male radio stars had some female that bounced their lines back to them. Hope found his in 16 year old Patricia Wilder, a Georgia belle who had run away from home to perform. He called her character Honey Chile because of her golden hair and thick Southern accent, and when the radio show ended, Honey Chile joined both the Hopes on a cross-country tour playing some of the large movie houses in the nation.

When Hope appeared in a 1934 comedy called *Going Spanish*, he thought so poorly of the movie that he joked, "When they catch John Dillinger, they're going to make him sit through it twice." But in spite of his previous bad experiences with the film industry, 1935 saw Warner Brothers hire Hope to do three short subject films. The first, *Old Grey Mayor*, was a typical Hollywood farce, but *Watch the Birdie* and *Double Exposure* allowed him more time to do what he did best: make wisecracks. He also appeared that year opposite Fanny Brice and Eve Arden in a new production of the Ziegfeld Follies. Meanwhile, Patricia Wilder left him to go out on her own, so a Dallas native named Margaret Johnson became the new Honey Chile in the *Atlantic White Flash Program* in January 1936.

Though Hope had performed in several movies and continued to toy with radio, by the end of the year he was back on Broadway, this time starring in *Red, Hot and Blue*. Though there was a significant internal strife and wrangling over the production, it received good reviews, and Hope enjoyed starring opposite one of his favorite actresses, Ethyl Merman. The production ran from October 1936 through April 10, 1937. That same spring, he landed his first big radio contract when he was hired to star in Woodbury Soap*'s Rippling Rhythm Review* on NBC out of New York. The show had begun as simply a musical showcase, but the sponsors from Woodbury Soap wanted to add some humor to the program, so they recruited Hope to join the cast. The Woodbury Show marked a change in Hope's attitude toward radio, as he would later recall, "I was doing a Broadway show and vaudeville in between. I saw a radio as promotion – as pure validity to build an audience for my stage for. But then the more I got into it I saw all the way it was going at it is the hot thing of the future – and – I really liked the money."

As always, he brought his own brand of self-deprecating humor to the show by often playing on the fact that it was sponsored by a company that made soap. For example, he used phrases like "I'm all lathered up" with his new Honey Chile, Claire Hazel, a young woman from South Carolina. While some people found Hope's humor to be a bit too "on the nose" for their case, *Variety* magazine praised the show, saying, "Bob Hope's addition as MC and funster appears just what the doctor ordered. Certainly his presence patches those lulls which have been bobbing up of late. Fashion in which Hope maneuvers the program, glibly filling in gaps and introducing number, definitely sets him up. Result was one of the swiftest moving Rippling stanzas in weeks. Hope added enough fresh chatter and gags to give the entire broadcast a lift."

While Hope was working in radio, Crosby was seemingly everywhere else. In addition to making records, Crosby's voice was also being heard in movies, especially the new musical comedies being made by Mack Sennett. These short subject films included such jewels as *One More Chance*, in which he appeared as Bing Bangs, and *Dream House*, in which he played a plumber named Bing Fawcett. In 1932, he appeared as Bing Hornsby in *The Big Broadcast*, the first film in which he received top billing.

After the success of *The Big Broadcast*, Crosby was offered roles in other films. The 1930s were the Golden Age of the big Hollywood musical, and there were not enough actors available who could also sing and dance. This put Crosby in a perfect position to rise to stardom, and rise he did. In 1933 alone, he starred in four films. In one, *College Humor*, he played Professor Frederick Danvers, a college professor competing with the football team's star a lovely young co-ed. In the 21st century, this may sound farfetched or even inappropriate, but it was a common theme during that time, because many new professors were only a few years older than their students. Also, as one writer observed, Crosby never seemed to be a serious threat to anyone, on or off screen: "Perhaps it is his uncompromising masculinity and obvious inability to overplay anything that made him so innocuous to his own sex. Unlike most of the other radio names, he never seems to be trying to be charming. The toothy smile, the Sunday School superintendent's function [play] no part in the Crosby technique. He borrows something from the old deadpan school of slapstick comedy and something from the insouciant ogle of the professional masher to produce an effect of being congenitally at home and sure of himself anywhere – not working hard in the least, just taking as it comes."

In 1934, Crosby starred in four more films, including *We're Not Dressing*, in which he played seaman Stephen Jones and Carole Lombard played his employer, a wealthy socialite. When they are stranded along with several of her friends on a desert island, no one knows what to do except Jones, and throughout the movie he saves them from starvation with a well-timed clambake and from boredom with his charming singing. In the end, Crosby and Lombard's characters are rescued and live happily ever after, making the movie a perfect tale at the height of the Great Depression.

When Crosby first came to CBS, he was asked to fill out a rather extensive biographical questionnaire, and one of the questions he was asked was, "What would you do if you had a million dollars?" His reply is insightful, given that at that time he'd likely never had a thousand dollars at one time: "If 1 million bucks ever came my way, I could doubtless distribute a considerable amount to relatives, etc., in loans, and still have enough....I'm pretty socialistic in this connection and really don't think anyone is entitled to or should have more than they need to live comfortably. My wants are comparatively simple... In point of fact, if I ever connect with the aforesaid amount, I'll wash up."

At the same time, Crosby was learning that while movies paid good money, they were also hard work. During the filming of one production in 1934, he wrote to a friend, "I am three weeks along into She Loves Me Not, a collegiate comedy with a couple of songs, from the play now current in New York. It has a terrific script, great dialogue, and grand situation. I don't see how it can fail to be a great laugh picture, and fine for me. I finish the picture in another week, the radio May 26th, and following this plan on resting for possibly a couple of months. Feeling a little tired, and further income in May & June will put me in a very disagreeable income tax bracket. So I might as well rest as give it back to Uncle Sam. I am trying to pick up a ranch near San Diego, not too elaborate, and if successful, you can come down and start me off right on some intensive gentleman farming."

Of course, Crosby would soon enough find out that having money was not so difficult for him after all, and as his fortunes increased, he began to enjoy many of the fruits of his labor. One of the first big expenditures he made was the purchase of a thoroughbred race horse in 1935, and two years later, he joined millionaire Charles Howard and his son Lindsey in founding the Del Mar Thoroughbred Club. The Del Mar Club ran the Del Mar Racetrack in Del Mar, California, and Crosby continued to serve on the club's board of directors for much of his life. Crosby and the Howards became such close friends that Bing even named his youngest son after Lindsey.

The two men also partnered to form the Binglin Stable in Moorpark, then a small hamlet in Ventura County, California, and they later bought a ranch in Argentina to breed and train horses to race at the Hipódromo de Palermo in Palermo, Buenos Aires. Some of the best horses were later moved to the United States, and one of these horses, Ligaroti, ran in a 1938 race against Charles Howard's best horse, the world famous Seabiscuit.

Crosby also spent much of 1935 making movies, the most important of which was *The Big Broadcast of 1936*. In it, he again played himself, just as he had in 1932, and this film proved to be an even bigger success, as audiences had been clamoring for more since the first *Big Broadcast* movie. Crosby also got to indulge his love for all things Southern while filming *Mississippi*, in which he played a pacifist turned riverboat entertainer.

Mississippi led to Crosby being cast in somewhere more dramatic roles, though in a comedic form. For example, in 1938's *Sing You Sinners*, he played one of three brothers trying to make it in show business, but he is the black sheep of the three and is always encouraging them to take underhanded short cuts. Eventually, by the end of the movie, he is reformed and goes straight.

Waikiki Wedding, released in 1937, gives some interesting insight into Crosby's personal character. In that movie, he worked with Anthony Quinn, himself also new in the business, and Quinn was a Hispanic who had experienced his fair share of prejudice already. However, he later noted that Crosby was ahead of his time is how he treated people of other ethnicities: "Bing was one of the most amazing people in the world because he had worked with so many minorities, and minorities were having a lot of trouble in those days…And Bing understood, he understood what I must have been going through and he was most helpful to me, his whole attitude. I always loved him because of the way he treated [people]. There was a shoeshine man at the entrance to the Paramount gate named Oscar. And Bing was one of his favorites because Bing came in and, I mean, he could talk the talk and he was wonderful at it. And Oscar and he would laugh, but there was nothing about Bing that was patronizing. He had worked with Louis and all the great musicians of the time and was used to being with blacks and Mexicans and all kinds of minorities. So he was actually wonderful to work with and made you at east, put me at my ease." *Waikiki Wedding* is also significant because it features the love song, "Sweet Leilani", a smooth romantic number that won Crosby his first Academy Award for Best Original Song.

Around the later years of the decade, Crosby's radio career began to expand while Hope looked to break into the movies. In 1936, Crosby replaced Paul Whiteman, the man who had once been his mentor, on the Kraft Music Hall, and he remained with this weekly radio program through the end of World War II. It was while working with this show that he debuted his signature song, debuting "Where the Blue of the Night (Meets the Gold of the Day)" during one of his famous "whistling interludes." Crosby was also using his newfound wealth to buy time to hone his golf game. He hosted the first National Pro-Am Golf Championship in 1937. Later known as the "Crosby Clambake," it was first held at the Rancho Santa Fe Golf Club in Rancho Santa Fe, California.

Meanwhile, even though he enjoyed his time on radio, Hope still had his eye on Hollywood and a career in motion pictures. Part of his dream was realized when he was cast in *The Big Broadcast Of 1938*, but he still realized he was far away from truly being a star, as evidenced by this anecdote: "When I set off the train in Pasadena, there was no block long limousine waiting to whisk Dolores and me to a mansion in Bel Air. No dancing starlets with masses of grapefruit. Not even a Red Cap with wilted gladiolus." In the movie, Hope was in many ways playing himself, because his character was a radio MC broadcasting from abroad. As it turned out, what they took from the movie was a song entitled "Thanks For the Memories," which would become one of his signature pieces for the rest of his career.

As the 1930s drew to a close, Hope's movie career remained stalled. He made three films in 1938, including *Thanks for the Memory*, which was written especially for him, and the following year he appeared in four more pictures, but none of them were memorable. In fact, far from being a critically acclaimed actor, the professional highlight of the year was when Hope was invited to host the Academy Awards, and though he would go on to host the prestigious awards show 13 more times over the next 4 decades, he would never win one himself. True to form, he would find new and funnier ways to make fun of this omission. Here are a few of his more famous remarks:

"Welcome to the Academy Awards -- or as it's known at my house, Passover."

"I've never wanted an Oscar, although they are reassuring to an actor who doesn't know how really great he is."

"We're all here to celebrate Oscar -- or as he's known at my house, The Fugitive!"

"Personally, I never drink on Oscar nights, as it interferes with my suffering."

"It's wonderful to be here in person. I couldn't be here in spirit, so I'm here in person."

As Hope continued to host the Academy Awards shows, some of the members clearly felt embarrassed that such an important person in the American entertainment world had never received an Oscar. To make up for it, the Academy would recognize his work every few years with honorary awards, beginning as early as 1940, when they recognized "his unselfish services to the motion picture industry." A few years later, in 1944, they gave him another "for his many services to the Academy." Then, in 1952, at the 25th Academy Awards, the members gave Hope an Honorary Award "for his contribution to the laughter of the world, his service to the motion picture industry, and his devotion to the American premise." In 1959, Hope received the Jean Hersholt Humanitarian Award for his service to others, and in 1965, the Academy gave him one final award "for unique and distinguished service to the industry and the Academy."

While in Hollywood, Hope continued to "call in" his radio show on the East Coast through a transcontinental hookup, and by the time he completed filming, he had a new 10 year contract with Pepsodent for his own show. *The Pepsodent Show Starring Bob Hope* aired on NBC on Tuesday nights and was soon the number one show in America. In addition to Hope, radio legends Jerry Colonna and Barbara Jo Allen were also regulars. Hope would continue to do the show for the next 18 years, and much of his success was due to the fact that he surrounded himself with excellent writers. He would later explain, "I believed I was the first of the comedians to hire several writers at a time. I think I was also the first to admit openly that I employed writers. In the early days of radio, comedians fostered the illusion that all of those funny sayings came right out of their own skulls."

Hope and Colonna in 1940

    With the money he was guaranteed by his Pepsodent contract, Bob decided to take Dolores on a long awaited vacation. Joined by his brother Jack, as well as Jack's new wife, the 4 of them departed from New York in early August 1939 and set sail for England. Unfortunately, it turned out they were picking the worst possible time to travel to Europe, because Hitler's invasion of Poland was just days away from starting World War II. They weren't the only ones stuck in Europe at the time either: "With the war imminent, Hollywood yesterday realized how many of its important stars are still in Europe. Tyrone Power...Charles Boyer...Robert Montgomery...Maureen O'Sullivan....Bob Hope, who planned a European holiday, is cutting his visit short to hurry home." While it must have been unnerving to travel the Atlantic just ahead of the Nazi invasion of Poland, it could not have hurt Hope's feelings to have his name linked with such stars as Tyrone Power and Maureen O'Sullivan.

Once they arrived back home, Bob and Dolores were in for another big surprise. After several years of trying, they learned that they would not be able to conceive, so shortly before they left for Europe, they had filed an application to adopt and were told to check back when they got home. As it turned out, the agency had good news for them; they were able to adopt their first child, a daughter they named Linda, before the year was finished. In 1946, they adopted three more kids: Tony, Kelly, and Nora.

The Hope family in 1956

Chapter 5: The Road Together

"Bing Crosby and I weren't the types to go around kissing each other. We always had a light jab for each other. One of our stock lines used to be "There's nothing I wouldn't do for Bing, and there's nothing he wouldn't do for me. And that's the way we go through life - doing nothing for

each other!" - Bob Hope

Hope and Crosby in *Road To Bali* (1952)

In 1940, Hope and Crosby made the first of what would become their signature movies. Known as the *Road to* movies, it was a series of seven films that they would make across two decades, all of which had the common theme of making fun of a popular genre of the time. The first, *Road to Singapore*, poked fun at the kind of romantic comedies that both Hope and Crosby were making at this time; they play two playboys who leave town to get away from romantic problems. Of course, their troubles only increase when they both fall for Dorothy Lamour. Lamour was actually Hope's choice for leading lady because he had worked with her on domestic USO tours and was impressed by both her professionalism and her flexibility. The latter was particularly important, since, as Hope would later say, "She stands there before the camera and ad libs with Bing Crosby and me, fully knowing the way the script's written, she'll come up second or third best." The movies were so popular that they were scheduled to start filming the eighth movie when Crosby died.

Hope and Lamour in *Road To Bali* (1952)

Not only was *Road to Singapore* wildly popular, but it also introduced the public to a number of sight gags that they would crave seeing again and again in future films. The first of these was "Pat-a-cake"; in this and future films, the two men would often play pat-a-cake to distract their opponents right before a fight broke out. Then there was the matter of Crosby's weight. While not even noticeably overweight by today's standards, much was made in the *Road to* movies of Crosby's expanding waistline. Finally, there were the cons. Though the men's characters were not initially con men, they developed the talent as the movie went on, and in most of the subsequent films in the series, they would be cheaters right from the beginning.

Not surprisingly, because of the popularity of *Road to Singapore*, Paramount was anxious to make another similar film, which led to the release of *Road to Zanzibar* in 1941. This film, a spoof of the safari films made popular by the Tarzan series, also borrowed humorous themes from 1939's hit, *Stanley and Livingston*. Not only did *Zanzibar* borrow jokes and musical styles from *Singapore*, but it did so unashamedly, and Crosby and Hope were now sufficiently confident in their own talents and each other's timing to introduce many ad libbed gags to the film. These factors set the stage for more *Road to ...* movies, including *Road to Morocco*, released the following year.

Road to Morocco proved to be the best *Road to...* picture yet, and this time the victim of its sarcastic barbs was the desert island film. Crosby and Hope play two con men stranded on an island following a shipwreck, but in something of a "gender bender" element, they are captured and sold as slaves to a beautiful princess played by Lamour. Not only was the film popular with the public, but it also became the first *Road to...* picture to also receive critical acclaim in the form of two Oscar nominations: one for Best Sound Recording and another for Best Writing, Original Screenplay. Decades later, it was chosen by the United States Library of Congress to be preserved in the National Film Registry, and it is also on the American Film Institute's "100 Years...100 Laughs" list. The theme song, "(We're Off on the) Road to Morocco", a duet by Crosby and Hope, even made the AFI's "100 Years...100 Songs" list.

In 1943, Hope and Crosby completed work on *Road to Utopia*, but by this time the United States was caught up in World War II and Paramount held off releasing the film until 1946. *Road to Utopia* is unique in comparison to the other *Road to...* pictures in various ways. For example, it is the only one of the movies not to mention a specific location in its title, and even though the destination was Alaska, it is called "utopia" in the movie. Also, while the other six pictures were set in their respective current eras, *Road to Utopia* was set at the turn of the 20th century. The film even poked fun at Paramount itself and film making in general.

For the time being, however, Hollywood stars were in a rush to support the war effort, either by fighting or performing, and in this regard, Crosby and Hope were no exceptions. They both put the *Road to...* movies on hold and devoted themselves to supporting the troops and their families at home.

For Crosby, this began with the release of his most popular song, "White Christmas", in 1941. He performed the somber piece over the radio on Christmas Day of 1941. While some might take issue with a secular piece being so popular, the fact it could not be claimed by just one faith certainly helped it do such a wonderful job of uniting the country. With the whole world at war, many were away from loved ones and in strange places for the first time, which is why so many of the song's lyrics were appealing to listeners.

Decca released the song as a single the following fall, just in time for the 1942 holiday season, and it rose to the top spot by Halloween and remained there until well into January. This time, sales were helped by the song being featured in Crosby's new movie, *Holiday Inn*, but Decca shrewdly continued to re-release it each year for 16 years. The song made it to the top of the charts in 1945, the first Christmas after the end of the war, and again in January 1947. Today, Guinness World Records still recognizes it as the best-selling single of all time, with over 50 million copies sold around the world. For his part, Crosby remained dubious about his part in the song's popularity, maintaining that "a jackdaw with a cleft palate could have sung it successfully." As it turned out, the first version was used so many times in ensuing years that Crosby was compelled to make a new version in 1947, and that one has been used ever since.

Crosby made few movies during the war years, instead opting for small guest appearances in a few feature length films, such as *Star Spangled Rhythm* and *Here Come the Waves*. He also starred in some obligatory short subjects in support of the war effort. However, he spent much of his time traveling around the world entertaining American servicemen. During his time in Europe, Crosby even learned to read German well enough to tape propaganda broadcasts for the Allies, and Nazi soldiers liked the sound of his voice so much that they even began to refer to him affectionately as "Der Bingle." By the end of the war, Crosby was even more popular among the American troops than his longtime partner, Bob Hope.

However, it was near the end of the war that Crosby played his most famous and important character, Father Chuck O'Malley. In *Going My Way* (1944), O'Malley was the type of priest most parishes dream of; young and enthusiastic, he was just as much at home on the baseball field as in the pulpit. The young people thought him hip, older members found him charming, and the priest is even able to win over his aging superior by raising funds for a new building. On top of all that, since the priest is played by Bing Crosby, he manages to be a world class singer too. In this case, the song was "Swinging on a Star," which won Crosby another Academy Award.

Both the American public and the critics loved Father O'Malley, perhaps because he gave his audience such a feel of optimism for the future. In addition to calling *Going My Way* the best film of Crosby's career, the *New York Times* review notes that designation is "saying a lot for a performer who has been one of the steadiest joys of the screen. But, in this Leo McCarey film,...he has definitely found his sturdiest role to date." The *Times*' critic, Bosley Crowther, said Crosby "has been stunningly supported by Barry Fitzgerald, who plays one of the warmest characters the screen has ever known. As a matter of fact, it is a cruel slight to suggest that this is Mr. Crosby's show. It is his and Mr. Fitzgerald's together. And they make it one of the rare delights of the year."

Hollywood rewarded Crosby's efforts in the film with his first Academy Award for Best Actor, and the film took home six more Oscars, including one for Best Picture. When accepting his Oscar, Crosby remained humble, saying, "This is the only country in the world where an old broken-down crooner can win an Oscar for acting. It shows that everybody in this country has a chance to succeed. I was just lucky enough to have Leo McCarey take me by the hand and lead me through the picture."

Not surprisingly, Crosby reprised his role the following year in *The Bells of St. Mary's* (1945), and this time, Father O'Malley tries to work with a beautiful but stern nun played by Ingrid Bergman. The two work out their differences in the end, while saving a parish school in the process. This film won Crosby another Oscar nomination, making Father O'Malley one of only four characters in Hollywood history to garner two Academy Award nominations in a row.

Crosby made two of his most important movies, but Hope was performing the kind of war service that would become his trademark. Like most Americans in December 1941, Hope felt that the country and lifestyle that he loved was in danger. In fact, his radio show was pre-empted for President Roosevelt's famous speech to Congress asking for a declaration of war after Pearl Harbor, and when he came back on the air a week later, he announced loud and clear his own plan for contributing to the war effort: "Good evening ladies and gentlemen…This is Bob Hope, and I just want to take a moment to say that last Tuesday night at this time I was sitting out there with you listening to our President as he asked all Americans to stand together in this emergency. We feel that in times like these – more than ever before, we need a moment of relaxation. All of us on the Pepsodent show will do our best to bring it to you. We think this is not a question of keeping up morale…. To most Americans, morale is taken for granted. There is no need to tell a nation to keep smiling when it's never stopped. It's that ability to laugh that make us the great people that we are…Americans! All of us in this studio feel that if we can bring into your homes a little of this laughter each Tuesday night we are helping to do our part."

Hope made few movies during the war years because he instead preferred to focus his energy on entertaining the men and women fighting overseas. He actually became aware of the power of laughter to comfort people under stress while he and Dolores were on their way back from their ill-fated trip to England. The ship they were on, the famous *RMS Queen Mary*, was overcrowded with passengers overwhelmed with concerns about their personal safety, loved ones on both sides of the Atlantic, and the future of the world in general. Hope offered to cheer them up with a special show, and in a move that would soon become his trademark, he concluded his performance with a version of "Thanks for the Memories", re-written especially for that occasion. The crowd loved it and thanked him for his comforting support. This also led to his idea of performing USO shows, beginning with his first one in California on May 6, 1941. Even though America had not yet joined the war, the men that he was entertaining knew they were potentially training for something bigger than just defending the homefront.

A few months later, when those men and thousands of others shipped out to Europe and the Pacific to fight in World War II, Hope knew that he wanted to go with them, and over the next 50 years, he would make a total of 57 overseas tours to entertain men fighting in Europe, Korea, Vietnam and the Middle East. A young war correspondent named John Steinbeck caught Hope's act in 1943 and reported, "When the time for recognition of service to the nation in wartime comes to be considered, Bob Hope should be high on the list. This man drives himself and is driven. It is impossible to see how he can do so much, can cover so much ground, can work so hard, and can be so effective. He works month after month at a pace that would kill most people."

Hope on a USO tour

Hope on a USO tour performing for soldiers during the Gulf War

For his part, Hope was humble about his role, mentioning in one routine, "Were the soldiers at the last camp happy to see me! They actually got down on their knees. What a spectacle! What a tribute! What a crap game!" But no soldier enjoyed the shows as much as he enjoyed doing them, as demonstrated by what he wrote about his experiences on tour: "We went right to work doing shows for small groups in one Quonset hut after another. They were a tough audience….They'd been there so long they didn't want to thaw out. … Most of them were from Alabama…but when those kids did finally warm up, it was terrific. We came out of one hut and there were about six hundred standing in the rain. We tried to do a show but if Tony had gotten out his guitar it would have shrunk…so we packed the whole six hundred guys in one Quonset hut that normally holds three hundred. Now I really know how it feels to play a packed house."

While Hope has become famous for his USO shows, it's often forgotten that he made his way to war zones and was thus putting his own personal safety at risk to perform during these travels. According to one correspondent, "One of the generals said Hope was a first rate military target since he was worth a division; that's about 15,000 men. Presumably the Nazis appreciated Hope's value, since they thrice bombed towns while the comic was there."

Hope meeting General George Patton in 1943

In addition to his USO tours, Hope did make some movies during the war, and naturally, most of them were of a patriotic nature, like *Strictly G.I.* in 1943 and *Hollywood Victory Caravan* in 1945. He also appeared as the Master of Ceremonies in *Star Spangled Rhythm* in 1942, a patriotic production that featured performances by many of Hollywood's biggest names, including Bing Crosby.

However, of all of Hope's movies made during the war, none stands out as much as *My Favorite Blond*. In this film, released in 1942, he played Larry Haines, an American vaudevillian who accidentally becomes involved with secret agents on both sides of the war in the days before Pearl Harbor. While there is no mention of his name in the credits, Bing Crosby also showed up for a few minutes in a cameo performance.

Once the war was over and the troops were coming home, Hope and Crosby finally found time to work together on more *Road to...* pictures. Following the release of *Road to Utopia* in 1946, the two began working on *Road to Rio*, and this time the victim of their sarcasm was the South American western. The movie was popular, but both men were busier than they had ever been before, so it would be several years before they could work a collaboration into their schedules, at least on screen, because the *Road to...* movies were not the only thing that Hope and Crosby collaborated on; in 1947, the two both bought shares in the Los Angeles Rams football team.

Crosby's interest in sports also extended to baseball, and he bought a part-ownership in the Pittsburgh Pirates baseball team in 1946. While the team would be a source of pleasure for the rest of his life, it was also a source of tremendous stress. For example, when the Pirates made it to a deciding game in the 1960 World Series, Crosby was too nervous to attend the game and instead flew to Paris to get as far away from the excitement as possible. He listened to the game on the radio, but he also arranged for NBC to record the game so that he could watch it when he returned. That recording of the broadcast, including the final walk-off home run, was later discovered in his wine cellar and broadcast in 2010.

Hope never owned part of a football team, but during his years on television, he regularly hosted specials for the College Football All-America Team, and the highlight of each special came when each player came on stage and introduced himself to Hope. The old man would then make some sort of crack about either the player or his school. In the meantime, Hope continued to make movies, albeit with mixed success. In 1947, he tried to follow up his success in *My Favorite Blond* with *My Favorite Brunette*. Told in flashbacks, Hope plays Ronnie Jackson, a baby photographer who has been framed for murder. Like the *Road to...* movies, it poked fun at a film genre, this time the *film noir* detective movies. Lamour starred with Hope in the picture, but Crosby only made another of his popular cameo appearances. The film was popular among audiences and critics alike, one of whom assured his readers, "This is a first rate Hope performance and Bob really has himself a time. So will you."

The following year, Hope made several more films, including *The Paleface*, in which he plays a cowardly dentist named "Painless" Peter Potter. When he is falsely accused of a heroic deed, his life actually changes for the worse. However, the highlight of the film is when Hope sings "Buttons and Bows", which not only became a best-selling hit but also won an Oscar for Best Song in 1948.

While Hope had a public persona as an all-American family man, the truth was quite a bit more complicated. Many in Hollywood knew him to be a womanizing skirt chaser who often cheated on his wife, making his cheating an open secret. Hope's affair with actress and fellow USO performer Marilyn Maxwell was so widely known that many in Hollywood took to calling her Mrs. Bob Hope.

Maxwell in the trailer for *Stand By for Action* (1942)

In 1949, Hope entered into his longest adulterous relationship when he met Barbara Payton, an aspiring actress and a divorcee with a bad reputation, in Dallas, Texas. Despite the red flags, Hope set her up in her own apartment in Hollywood and kept her was his mistress for a few months before he tired of her. At that point, he paid her to leave quietly. Seven years later, after she had married and divorced a third time, Payton lost custody of her only child and then married a fourth time. Payton sold the story of her relationship with Hope to a tabloid style magazine, but Hope followed his advisors' recommendations to ignore the story, and it soon died down. Payton herself died 10 years later after years of drug and alcohol abuse.

Crosby with Perry Como and Arthur Godfrey in 1950

"[Crosby saw] an enormous advantage in prerecording his radio shows. The scheduling could now be done at the star's convenience. He could do four shows a week, if he chose, and then take a month off. But the networks and sponsors were adamantly opposed. The public wouldn't stand for 'canned' radio, the networks argued. There was something magic for listeners in the fact that what they were hearing was being performed and heard everywhere, at that precise instant. Some of the best moments in comedy came when a line was blown and the star had to rely on wit to rescue a bad situation. Fred Allen, Jack Benny, Phil Harris, and also Crosby were masters at this, and the networks weren't about to give it up easily." – John Dunning, author of *On the Air: The Encyclopedia of Old-Time Radio*

Crosby was always aware that much of his success in music and films came as a result of the unique time in history in which he was born. For one thing, he barely missed a full-blown vaudeville career, and he came around at just the right time to have his singing career launch as radio was growing more popular. At the same time, he came to radio late enough in the game to have the use of some new types of microphones that others who came before him never got to use. This coincidence of time and technology allowed him to develop his own unique approach to singing, combining a soft, gentle tone with the ability to shake things up by bending notes and off key tones in the way of an old time jazz musician. As his career progressed, he was also able to pass what he had learned on to others.

Wartime often brings the development of new technology, and World War II was no exception. While the advances were used almost exclusively by the military during the war, it soon became available to corporations following the war, and Crosby had actually had a chance to work with technology in Europe that hadn't made its way to America during the war. One of these was the tape recorder, a new device that allowed actors and singers to record their performances to be played over the air at a later time. Crosby, who had always been interested in the science of production, formed The Crosby Research Foundation after the war to find new ways to refine the recording and playing devices for use by entertainers.

Over the years, the foundation hired many of the best men in the field, and as a result it obtained a number of patents for their discoveries. Among their most popular developments was the "laugh track", a concept still used on television and radio today. Jack Mullin, who worked with Crosby, explained how the laugh track came about and helped Crosby's shows, "One time Bob Burns, the hillbilly comic, was on the show, and he threw in a few of his folksy farm stories, which of course were not in Bill Morrow's script. Today they wouldn't seem very off-color, but things were different on radio then. They got enormous laughs, which just went on and on. We couldn't use the jokes, but Bill asked us to save the laughs. A couple of weeks later he had a show that wasn't very funny, and he insisted that we put in the salvaged laughs. Thus the laugh-track was born."

Crosby explained the importance of some of the technology that he began to use in the mid-1940s, "By using tape, I could do a thirty-five or forty-minute show, then edit it down to the twenty-six or twenty-seven minutes the program ran. In that way, we could take out jokes, gags, or situations that didn't play well and finish with only the prime meat of the show; the solid stuff that played big. We could also take out the songs that didn't sound good. It gave us a chance to first try a recording of the songs in the afternoon without an audience, then another one in front of a studio audience. We'd dub the one that came off best into the final transcription. It gave us a chance to ad lib as much as we wanted, knowing that excess ad libbing could be sliced from the final product. If I made a mistake in singing a song or in the script, I could have some fun with it, then retain any of the fun that sounded amusing." Mullin noted, "In the evening, Crosby did the whole show before an audience. If he muffed a song then, the audience loved it – thought it was very funny – but we would have to take out the show version and put in one of the rehearsal takes. Sometimes, if Crosby was having fun with a song and not really working at it, we had to make it up out of two or three parts. This ad lib way of working is commonplace in the recording studios today, but it was all new to us."

In 1947, Crosby invested $50,000 of his own money in the Ampex Company, which at that time was developing the first commercial quality reel-to-reel tape recorder in North America. He was still working for NBC at this time and tried to convince them to purchase some of the new equipment so that he could record some of his shows in bulk for later broadcast. When NBC refused, he left them and went to work for ABC instead. ABC was open to new technology, so it allowed Crosby to become the first radio performer to ever pre-record his shows and commercial spots.

This was an amazing improvement for a number of reasons. For one, as recording allowed performers to tape several shows at one time, freeing them to pursue other career opportunities while keeping their radio commitments. Also, when recording a performance or show ahead of time, performers and producers were able to work together to create a more flawless production. This was becoming increasingly important because motion pictures were constantly setting a higher standard of perfection in the minds of audiences. Finally, recording allowed several performers to appear on the same show, even when they were unable to align their personal schedules.

Not one to keep good news to himself, Crosby gave an Ampex Model 200, one of the first produced, to his friend Les Paul. Though a professional musician, Paul also had a scientific bent and tinkered with the machine until he invented multitrack recording. This allowed different members of the same band or choir to record their parts on separate tapes that could then be adjusted for maximum effect by a musical technician. Crosby continued to support advances in recording and persuaded Frank Sinatra to join him in building the now well-known United Western Recorders studio in Los Angeles.

One of the things that made Crosby able to exert such influence on the radio industry was his own popularity. The same soldiers who had voted him their favorite performer during the war were now returning home to a prosperous America where they could afford luxury high-quality radios and phonographs. They were also getting married and starting families that gathered around the radio in the evening. In 1940s and 50s America, Dad decided what was listened to at night, and many fathers liked to listen to Bing Crosby. In 1948, several polls taken in America described him as "the most admired man alive." That same year, *Music Digest*, a well-respected industry magazine, reported that recordings of Bing Crosby took up more than half of all radio time allocated for music.

Crosby was a master at using his own popularity to influence the expectations of the American public. For instance, in 1950 he appeared in *Mr. Music*. While not an important film in its own right, the movie features a scene in which Crosby sings into one of his new Ampex tape recorders, and since the sound was excellent, the audience was introduced to a new way to enjoy music. Likewise, Crosby used his friendship with Bob Hope to convince Hope to begin recording some of his radio spots also.

Meanwhile, a decade after Crosby made his way into Christmas lore with his 1941 rendition of "White Christmas", Hope carved out a similar place for himself with "Silver Bells." While "Silver Bells" would never be as popular or as closely associated with one performer as "White

Christmas" was with Crosby, it is still a haunting melody that turns up every year during the Christmas season, and while Crosby's song appeals to a more nostalgic longing for peace and the past, "Silver Bells" is obviously written for the post-World War II era consumer culture. Though it's often forgotten today, the song came from Hope's 1951 film, *The Lemon Drop Kid*, in which he plays the title role of a gambler on the run from the mob. Like it sounds, it wasn't exactly a holiday film, nor is it remembered much today, but the song is still instantly recognizable and popular today.

In 1952, Hope starred in *Son of Paleface* as his previous character's son, and like the earlier movie, this film is a lighthearted romp through the Old West. While American audiences were not very fond of it, the audiences in Great Britain flocked to see it, making it the third most popular movie there that year.

By that time, Crosby was getting more involved with television, and in turn, he pushed for the development of a video recording device also. When Crosby made his television debut on *The Fireside Theatre* in 1950, the video recorders didn't exist yet, so he had to film his weekly show at the Hal Roach Studios. These "telefilms" were then sent out to television studios nationwide. In order to facilitate the development of the videotape, Crosby founded Bing Crosby Enterprises and hired the best experts available to develop the technology. The scientist he chose worked fast enough that by the end of 1951, the first videotape recording machine had been completed. Though the initial image was too blurry and fuzzy to be used effectively, it was a start. It would be several decades before VCRs became part of American homes, but television studios would have the ability to record their programs much sooner thanks in large part to Bing Crosby.

Realizing that if he was going to be part of the television industry, he was going to want to have some control over the product, Crosby formed a group of investors and purchased KCOP – TV in 1954. Five years later, he teamed up with another corporation to purchase KPTV.

Chapter 7: On the Road and Off Again

"I can't drink like Marvin, grunt like Steiger, enunciate like Olivier. And when it comes to Burton, I'm really in trouble." – Bob Hope

"Honestly, I think I've stretched a talent which is so thin it's almost transparent over a quite unbelievable term of years." - Bing Crosby

In 1951, Crosby starred in *Here Comes the Groom*, which was directed by Frank Capra and featured the charming number "In the Cool, Cool, Cool of the Evening." While the film was not particularly memorable, the song won Crosby yet another Academy Award. One of the next movies he made was *Road to Bali*, released in 1952. The American people by this time were hungry for a new *Road to…* movie, and Crosby, Hope and Lamour were happy to provide one. Unlike the previous five *Road to…* movies, *Road to Bali* was filmed in color and also featured cameo appearances by other popular stars of the day, including Jerry Lewis, Dean Martin, Jane

Russell, and Humphrey Bogart. It also contained numerous comic references to its Australian location. As it turned out, *Road to Bali* would be the last *Road to...* movie to star Dorothy Lamour, and it would also be the last one audiences would see for another decade.

Hope, Crosby and Lamour in *Road To Bali*

Sadly, it was not long after the release of *Road to Bali* that Bing learned his wife was dying of ovarian cancer. Their 22 year marriage had been a stormy one, with Bing often gone from home on movie sets or radio studios, and Dixie had often been left home alone with four little boys. At some point in time in the early years of their marriage, she had begun to drink socially in order to keep a closer eye on Bing's alcohol consumption, and ironically, while he mostly kicked his drinking problem, she eventually became an alcoholic. By the time her cancer was discovered, her body had been weakened by years of heavy drinking and had little to fight back with. Dixie died in September 1952. Making matters worse, Bing was forced to sell his share of Binglin Stables to pay the inheritance taxes levied by the state and federal government on his wife's estate. In turn, the Del Mar Racetrack created the Bing Crosby Breeder's Cub in his honor.

Bing's relationship with his four oldest sons, by this time all in their teens, has been the subject of much speculation, mostly because his oldest son, Gary, wrote a tell-all exposé, *Going My Own*

Way, in 1983. In the book, which intentionally invoked Bing's most famous movie, Gary accused his father of being both distant and cruel, if not outright abusive:

> "We had to keep a close watch on our actions...When one of us left a sneaker or pair of underpants lying around, he had to tie the offending object on a string and wear it around his neck until he went off to bed that night. Dad called it 'the Crosby lavalier'. At the time the humor of the name escaped me...
>
> 'Satchel Ass' or 'Bucket Butt' or 'My Fat-assed Kid'. That's how he introduced me to his cronies when he dragged me along to the studio or racetrack... By the time I was ten or eleven he had stepped up his campaign by adding lickings to the regimen. Each Tuesday afternoon he weighed me in, and if the scale read more than it should have, he ordered me into his office and had me drop my trousers... I dropped my pants, pulled down my undershorts and bent over. Then he went at it with the belt dotted with metal studs he kept reserved for the occasion. Quite dispassionately, without the least display of emotion or loss of self-control, he whacked away until he drew the first drop of blood, and then he stopped. It normally took between twelve and fifteen strokes. As they came down I counted them off one by one and hoped I would bleed early...
>
> When I saw *Going My Way* I was as moved as they were by the character he played. Father O'Malley handled that gang of young hooligans in his parish with such kindness and wisdom that I thought he was wonderful too. Instead of coming down hard on the kids and withdrawing his affection, he forgave them their misdeeds, took them to the ball game and picture show, taught them how to sing. By the last reel, the sheer persistence of his goodness had transformed even the worst of them into solid citizens. Then the lights came on and the movie was over. All the way back to the house I thought about the difference between the person up there on the screen and the one I knew at home."

Conversely, Bing's younger son Philip remembered his father in a very different way, as a kind, loving man who enjoyed taking his boys to the movie lot with him: "My dad was not the monster my lying brother said he was; he was strict, but my father never beat us black and blue, and my brother Gary was a vicious, no-good liar for saying so. I have nothing but fond memories of Dad, going to studios with him, family vacations at our cabin in Idaho, boating and fishing with him. To my dying day, I'll hate Gary for dragging Dad's name through the mud. He wrote *Going My Own Way* out of greed. He wanted to make money and knew that humiliating our father and blackening his name was the only way he could do it. He knew it would generate a lot of publicity. That was the only way he could get his ugly, no-talent face on television and in the newspapers. My dad was my hero. I loved him very much. He loved all of us too, including Gary. He was a great father."

In reality, both of the boys were probably somewhat right and somewhat wrong. Perhaps Gary as the oldest saw his father in the worst light, during the days of his heavy drinking, while the younger sons enjoyed a more settled and experienced father. No matter what the boys later said about him, Bing realized pretty quickly that he was going to have to find another mother for them, and to that end, he began to look around Hollywood for a new wife. One of the women that he spotted was a beautiful blonde named Grace Kelly, who he worked with in *The Country Girl* in 1953. In this, one of his most dramatic films, Crosby plays a washed up musician with a severe alcohol problem, and the exquisite Grace Kelly stars as his tragic, long suffering wife. Not only would *The Country Girl* win Kelly her only Oscar for Best Actress, it would also net Crosby his third Academy award nomination. Bing would later say about Kelly, "She's a great lady, with great talent and kind, considerate, friendly with everybody. She was great with the crew and they all loved her."

Grace Kelly

That same year, Crosby completed work on what ended up being his most popular movie, *White Christmas*. A sequel to 1942's *Holiday Inn*, the movie would go on to gross $30 million that year.

Crosby in the trailer of *White Christmas*

Banking on the popularity of a good spoof, Hope starred in *Casanova's Big Night* in 1954, a thinly veiled mockery of the historical adventure film. In the movie, he played a poor tailor posing as the world's greatest lover, but he soon learns that the great lover is also a great debtor and thus has to find a way to lose all his creditors before the film is over. Like most of Hope's films of this era, *Casanova's Big Night* opened to only lukewarm reviews.

Hope's next film, *The Seven Little Foys*, fared somewhat better, thanks in large part to James Cagney reprising his role as George M. Cohen in an excellent tap dancing sequence, but even though the movie was a hit, doing *The Seven Little Foys* made Hope nervous. He later confided, "The biggest challenge about doing *Foys* was that for the first time I had to play a real-life character and one that the public knew, and having to do some pretty heavy scenes. I wanted to get inside Eddie Foy as much as I could, so I read everything I could find, and even studied some old silent films he had made. Luckily, we had help from Brian and Charley Foy – and Eddie Jr. agreed to be a technical advisor on the project." Hope would later host a TV version of the movie on January 24, 1964 for *Bob Hope Presents The Chrysler Theatre.*

By this point in his life, Hope was able to spend more time working on his golf game than working on his act, becoming so good at golf that he played with just a four handicap. He also devoted much of his spare time to hosting tournaments to raise money for good causes, often hosting more than 100 tournaments each year and sometimes as many as 150. There was never a problem getting people to participate, as his personal skills and sense of humor made him an attractive member for any foursome.

Hope wasn't the only one in a state of transition during the middle of the decade. While the public still loved hearing Crosby sing, he himself was no longer so sure of his talent. In 1954, he told one reporter, " I don't sing anywhere as good as I used to, and I feel sincerely that it's getting worse. I don't see any purpose in trying to stretch something out that was once acceptable and that now is merely adequate, if that. I don't know what the reason for this condition is, unless it's apathy. I just don't have the interest in singing. I am not keen about it anymore. Songs all sound alike to me, and some of them so shoddy and trivial. I don't mean I didn't sing some cheap songs in the old days, but I had such a tremendous interest in singing and was so wrapped up in the work that it didn't matter. I don't know how to diagnose the condition, but it seems to me that possibly this apathy, this lack of desire, when I have to go to a recording session, transmits itself into nervous exhaustion and fatigue."

That said, it's likely that Crosby's words were born more out of depression following the loss of his wife than any real loss of talent. In tracking Crosby's singing career, Pleasants wrote, "[T]he octave B flat to B flat in Bing's voice at that time [1930s] is, to my ears, one of the loveliest I have heard in forty-five years of listening to baritones, both classical and popular, it dropped conspicuously in later years. From the mid-1950s, Bing was more comfortable in a bass range while maintaining a baritone quality, with the best octave being G to G, or even F to F. In a recording he made of 'Dardanella' with Louis Armstrong in 1960, he attacks lightly and easily on a low E flat. This is lower than most opera basses care to venture, and they tend to sound as if they were in the cellar when they get there."

Crosby's abilities shone prominently in his 1956 classic, *High Society*. In this charming tale Crosby again teamed up with Grace Kelly, this time playing an ex-husband who returns home on the eve of her marriage to someone else. Having been kicked out of her wealthy family years before because he was an entertainer, he is now determined to win her back before it is too late. Of course, everyone lives happily ever after, especially after Crosby charms them with a duet of "Now You Has Jazz" with Louis Armstrong.

By this time, Kelly had made it clear that, while she enjoyed working with Crosby, she was not interested in marrying him. Eventually, he remarried to 24 year old Kathryn Grandstaff. Like Dixie Lee before her, Kathryn gave up any plans she had for a career when the two married in 1957, instead focusing her time and attention to parenting Bing's four boys and three more children of her own. Harry was born in 1958, Mary Frances in 1959, and Nathaniel in 1961.

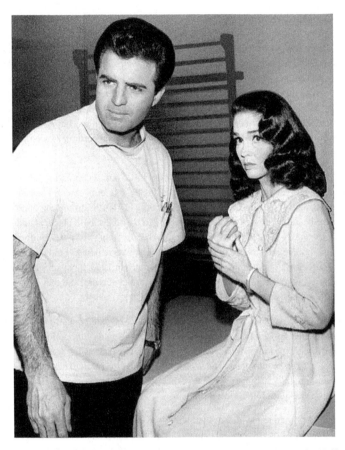

Kathryn Crosby and Vincent Edwards on the set of *Ben Casey* in 1965

As the 1950s wore on, Hope spent more and more time filming television specials and less time working on movies, so much so that his last popular picture was *The Road to Hong Kong* (1962). This was the last of the *Road to...* movies that he and Crosby would make, but unlike the previous six films, *The Road to Hong Kong* was not produced by Paramount. Instead, it was made in Great Britain, and Joan Collins played the type of role traditionally held by Dorothy Lamour (though Lamour did make a brief cameo appearance). This film is also unique among the *Road to...* movies because it is told in flashbacks by Joan Collins' character, but like the other movies in the series, it spoofs a popular genre, in this case the Russian spy movie.

One of the reasons Hope's film career was coming to an end was that he was well into his 50s, and thus no longer in line for romantic leads, even in comedies. Seeing the writing on the wall, he turned his attention to television, an increasingly popular medium. Indeed, this proved to be an excellent decision, because television would ultimately be the place where he made his biggest mark as an entertainer.

Hope had been under contract with NBC since 1934, but beginning in April 1950, they began to have him focus his time on making periodic television specials for their network. Television was still in its infancy at this time, and Hope would be one of the performers who would shape its future. One of the ways in which he did this was by using cue cards, which helped him appear relaxed and at ease on stage because he did not have to worry about what he would say next. Hope's shows were also popular with automobile and gas manufacturers, ensuring that over the next several decades, he would be sponsored by General Motors, Chrysler and Texaco.

By far, the most popular shows were Hope's Christmas specials, which would always feature pretty young actresses who would sing "Silver Bells" with him in duet. Through the years, he performed with everyone from Barbara Eden to Olivia Newton-John and Brooke Shields. To make the programs more appealing to families, he also occasionally brought his wife Dolores on stage to sing with him.

Hope was also popular enough to be fearless when it came to political humor. Eve at the height of the Red Scare and McCarthyism, Hope joked, "I have it on good authority that McCarthy is going to disclose the names of two million Communists. He has just got his hands on the Moscow telephone directory." He also knew that most Americans were big enough to laugh at themselves, even if one of them was the President of the United States: "Eisenhower admitted that the budget can't be balanced, and McCarthy said the Communists are taking over. You don't know what to worry about these days - whether the country will be overthrown or overdrawn."

While Hope was accustomed to making political jokes in America, he learned that not all national leaders had such good senses of humor. In 1958, he got permission from the State Department to visit and perform in Russia, but once there, however, he soon realized that he would have to get his personal style of humor past national censors. When they objected to his cracks about Sputnik, he had to explain to his interrogators: "We are anxious to cooperate but we must be reasonable. Satellites and missiles are a big topic in Russia just as they are in America. We both lose if we treat you any differently than any other country in the world. Listen, here are the jokes I told on my last television show: 'I guess you heard the big news from Cape Canaveral. Our government launched another submarine...'" Not only did his Russian hosts laugh, they allowed him to keep most of his act intact.

During election years, Hope was careful to remain bipartisan, which he accomplished by making fun of both parties' politicians. For example, in a special aired during the 1960 race between John F. Kennedy and Richard Nixon, Hope went after Kennedy's age and Nixon's honesty, both of which would be called into question during their terms in office: "A few months ago Kennedy's mother said, 'You have a choice. Do you want to go to camp this year or run for president?'…"Nixon lives here in Whittier, California. They're so sure he's going to be president they're building the log cabin he was born in."

Fortunately, Hope's humor was so good-natured that presidents were rarely insulted, which was made all the more important by the fact that he liked to have at least one past or current president at each of his Bob Hope Classics, founded by him in 1960. Until recently, this tournament was the only one on the PGA tour to last five rounds, and the event reached its high point in 1995, when Hope played in a foursome with Gerald Ford, George H.W. Bush, and Bill Clinton. This was the only time in history that three presidents played in the same golf foursome.

Like Hope, by the time Bing married Kathryn in the later stages of the 1950s, he was 54 years old and finding work in the movies harder to get. In 1959, he reprised his role as a priest, playing Father Conroy in *Say One For Me*. *Say One For Me* was almost like art imitating life, as Father Conroy was the priest for a parish full of actors and singers, much like the people Crosby himself worked with every day. The film features a number of solid musical pieces, as well as some decent acting, but it's not remembered as Crosby's best work.

As a father, Crosby was only too aware of the changes sweeping through the music industry in the late 1950s and early 60s, but he remained philosophical about the change, once saying of Elvis Presley, "He helped to kill off the influence of me and my contemporaries, but I respect him for that. Because music always has to progress, and no-one could have opened the door to the future like he did." He also ruefully joked about Sinatra, "Frank is a singer who comes along once in a lifetime, but why did he have to come in mine?" But for a while, Crosby thought that he might be able to keep up with some of the changes. In 1960, he starred with teen heartthrob Fabian in *High Time*, and that movie, his last collegiate comedy, brought him full circle in the world of college campus films. Decades earlier, he had played a student, then a young professor, and now he was the old guy on campus who just didn't quite fit in. As his career in music was winding down, the musical world rushed to honor him one more time by giving him a Lifetime Achievement Grammy in 1962. The following year, he was awarded the first ever Grammy Global Achievement Award.

In many ways, Bing's last hurrah in features films was *The Road to Hong Kong*. Released in 1962, it would be the last of the *Road to…* movies that he and Hope would make, but unlike the previous six films, *The Road to Hong Kong* was not produced by Paramount. Instead, it was made in Great Britain, and Joan Collins played the type of role traditionally held by Dorothy Lamour (though Lamour did make a brief cameo appearance). This film is also unique among the *Road to…* movies because it is told in flashbacks by Joan Collins' character, but like the other movies in the series, it spoofs a popular genre, in this case the Russian spy movie.

Crosby's final feature film was the 1966 remake of John Ford's *Stagecoach*, and it's hard to understand why he chose to be in this dramatic, non-musical movie. Certainly, a drunken doctor called upon to deliver a baby while under attack by Native Americans was not the type of role that he usually played. It is possible, perhaps, that he was considering continuing his career as an actor, even though his voice would no longer stand up under the pressure of making a musical. For whatever reason that he chose it, *Stagecoach* was almost predestined to fail, as the original was just too much of a classic for a remake to compete with.

Chapter 8: Turning to Television

"They said I was worth $500 million. If I was worth that much, I wouldn't have visited Vietnam, I'd have sent for it." – Bob Hope

Following his retirement from making features films, Crosby turned his attention towards television. In 1964, his own Bing Crosby Productions worked with the famous Desilu Studios to produce *The Bing Crosby Show*. However, it was on ABC for just one season because it failed to appeal to the new, younger television audiences. That said, Crosby Productions went on to produce several other successful shows, including the medical drama *Ben Casey* and the often maligned World War II comedy *Hogan's Heroes*. Crosby Productions even produced a game show called *Beat the Odds*.

At the same time, Hope was in his 60s, and beginning to receive awards recognizing his contribution to entertainment. Of the 2,000 plus awards and honors he would receive during his lifetime, none pleased him as much as those given by his country. In 1963, he received the Congressional Gold Medal from President John F. Kennedy, and six years later, President Lyndon Johnson awarded him the Presidential Medal of Freedom in recognition of his work with the USO. In 1980, he became the only civilian to receive Order of the Sword from the United States Air Force.

However, the Vietnam War proved to be a difficult time for Hope. He had spent every Christmas since the beginning of World War II with American troops around the world, bringing a little bit of home and laughs to them during the season, but he never went alone because he could count on other actors and actresses to join him on his tours. During Vietnam, however, many in Hollywood opposed America's involvement in the war, so he found it more difficult to find those willing to put their lives and careers on the line by going with him. Many of them also objected because the Department of Defense helped sponsor the entertainment, and they did not want to be seen as supporting the war effort.

For his part, Hope did not understand their reluctance. To him, the young men and women sitting on the ground in mud and blood stained fatigues in Vietnam were no less noble than their fathers had been a generation before. After he was almost killed by a Vietcong attack in 1967, one biographer noted, "Hope was mystified, and was growing increasingly intolerant of the pockets of dissent. Draft-card burnings on college campuses angered him... 'Can you imagine,' Hope wrote in a magazine article, '... that people in America are burning their draft cards to show their opposition and that some of them are actually rooting for your defeat?' To Hope it was inconceivable that his arguments on behalf of American GIs who were in southeast Asia helping to stem a Communist takeover would not be shared by every patriotic citizen..." To be fair, Hope never had a problem with sincere conscientious objectors. Back during World War II, he had come out publically in support of a fellow actor who refused to fight, saying, "...I admire [Lew] Ayres for his stand. It took courage to do that. It's against his religion to kill folks. He's volunteered for the Medical Corps – and it takes courage to go into the front lines and care for people."

While some opposed Hope's service to the military, most Americans did not, as attested to by the fact that both his 1970 and 1971 Christmas specials, filmed on a military base in South Vietnam, are among the top 50 most popular prime-time shows in American history. Each one garnered more than 60 percent of the share of viewers for their respective time slots. Not only were the servicemen grateful to the USO for bringing Hope to them, Hope was grateful for the opportunity to serve. When he completed his memoir, *The Last Christmas Show*, he dedicated it to "the men and women of the armed forces and to those who also served by worrying and waiting." He also donated all the money he made from the book to the USO.

Hope would ultimately his last overseas Christmas special in 1990, at the age of 87. The show was from Saudi Arabia, where life on American military bases was different from what he had experienced in the past. According to one biographer, "There were so many restrictions. Hope's jokes were monitored by the State Department to avoid offending the Saudis... and for the first time in Hope's memory, the media was restricted from covering the shows... Because in Saudi Arabia national custom prescribes that women must be veiled in public, Ann Jillian, Marie Osmond, and the Pointer Sisters were left off Hope's Christmas Eve show." The highlight for Hope may have been when Dolores, there with her husband for his last hurrah, sang "White Christmas" while standing on an armored vehicle. Not only was this the most popular Christmas song of all time, it was also the favorite number of their old friend Bing Crosby.

Chapter 9: Crosby's Final Years

Crosby and his family in a Christmas special in 1974

"He was an average guy who could carry a tune." – Bing Crosby's epitaph

In addition to working in production, Crosby also tried his hand at a few made-for-TV movies during the early 1970s. While none of these were memorable, it did give him some unique opportunities. For instance, in 1970's *Swing Out, Sweet Land*, he had the unique experience of portraying the great American comedian Mark Twain.

In 1974, Crosby contracted a nearly fatal fungal infection in his right lung, and after beating it, he decided to once again try recording and performing concerts. Unfortunately, there was not a big audience by this time for either his records or his performances, so he returned to what he had already mastered: the television special. In March 1977, CBS invited him to tape a special concert to commemorate his 50 years in entertainment, and many of his best friends were there that night, as was Bob Hope. After a triumphant evening of performing, Crosby was backing his way off the stage when he accidentally fell into the orchestra pit. He severely injured his back and had to remain hospitalized for a month before he was released. Ever the trooper, he returned to performing in August, but that performance also ended poorly when the power went out and he was forced to complete the concert without a microphone.

Crosby in London in 1977. Picture by Allan Warren

It's often said in show business that performers should always leave crowds wanting more, and unlike most of his peers, Bing Crosby accomplished this, albeit in a tragic way. He filmed his final TV show in London in September 1977, and in keeping with his love for the holiday, it was a Christmas special. However, this was one special that the world would never forget. In one of the most unique performances ever conceived, the king of the crooners teamed with rock star David Bowie in a duet of "The Little Drummer Boy" and "Peace on Earth." The producers rushed the single through production so that it could be released in time for Christmas. Not only was the single a hit in 1977, the duets themselves are considered by many to be one of the most memorable moments in television history.

Sadly, Crosby would not live to see his final triumph. After completing the Christmas special taping, he gave a few more public performances around Great Britain and then flew to Spain to enjoy some sun and golf. He hoped to rest up in preparation for beginning filming on an eighth *Road to...* movie. Rumor had it that it would be called *The Road to the Fountain of Youth* and would be modeled on the popular Monty Python movies. However, in the early evening of October 14, 1977, Bing Crosby suffered a massive heart attack after completing 18 holes of golf in Madrid. Those who were near him when he died claimed that his last words were, "That was a great game of golf, fellas." The following year, Crosby was posthumously honored by the United States Gold Association with the Bob Jones Award, and he was also inducted into the World Golf Hall of Fame.

Following his death, Kathryn had his body returned to America, and he was buried at the Holy Cross Cemetery in Culver City, California at sunrise on October 18. In keeping with his final wishes, only his immediate family, Bob Hope, Phil Harris and Rosemary Clooney attended. A new young reporter named Geraldo Rivera, sent by ABC to cover the burial, fittingly noted that it was just the time when "the blue of the night meets the gold of the day."

Crosby left behind a professional record that any performer would envy. He is one of only 22 performers to have three stars on the Hollywood Walk of Fame. The first, for music, was certainly well deserved. Crosby had 41 number one hit singles, and from 1931-1954, he had a record on the charts every year. From the standpoint of sales, he was the most successful musician of both the 1930s and 1940s.

The second star was for his work in radio. He is also a member of both the Radio and Popular Music Halls of Fame, as well as the Hit Parade Hall of Fame and even the Western Music Hall of Fame.

The third star was for his film career. According to estimates, viewers purchased over 1 trillion tickets to see his movies, which would make him the third most popular actor in history. Either way, from 1944-1948, he was the biggest box office draw in the world.

Of all the praise that Crosby received through the years, perhaps none was as poignant as that given by his best friend, Bob Hope. In 1990, Hope wrote of Crosby in his own autobiography, "Dear old Bing. As we called him, the Economy-sized Sinatra. And what a voice. God I miss that voice. I can't even turn on the radio around Christmas time without crying anymore."

Chapter 10: A Century of Laughs

"I've always been in the right place and time. Of course, I steered myself there." – Bob Hope

"I don't feel old. In fact, I don't feel anything until noon. Then it's time for my nap." – Bob Hope

Now in the twilight of his life and career, Hope's main focus turned to philanthropy. He also spent much of his time attending events held in his honor. In 1983, his 80th birthday celebration was held on air at the Kennedy Center in Washington, D.C. Not only was President Ronald Reagan and his wife Nancy, there, but so were most of the big names in television comedy, including Lucille Ball and George Burns among many others. Hope returned to the Kennedy Center in 1985 to receive a Life Achievement Award during the *Kennedy Center Honors*.

Hope receiving an award in 1978.

More honors came from overseas when Queen Elizabeth II made him an honorary Knight Commander of the Most Excellent Order of the British Empire in 1998. As always, he remained humble in the face of praise, saying "What an honor and what a surprise for a boy born in England, raised in Cleveland and schooled in vaudeville."

Though retired from regular acting, Hope remained active well into his 90s, and even as his failing eyesight made it more difficult to read cue cards, he still appeared in his own birthday special, *Bob Hope: the First 90 Years*, in 1993. The show appealed to a nostalgic audience and was a big hit, even winning an Emmy for Outstanding Variety, Music or Comedy Special. A few years later, Hope decided not to renew his contract with NBC, bringing to an end their 60 year relationship. His last special for them was called *Laughing with the Presidents*, which featured his personal recollections of American presidents he had known, from Franklin Roosevelt through Bill Clinton. The broadcast bombed, and Hope made only one more formal television appearance, at the Primetime Emmy Awards in 1997.

That same year, Hope was made an "Honorary Veteran" by the United States Congress, and when receiving his citation from President Bill Clinton, Hope said, "I've been given many awards in my lifetime — but to be numbered among the men and women I admire most — is the greatest honor I have ever received."

Many people at funerals say a person died before their time, and in the case of Bob Hope, this proved to be more than just a line. In 1998, the Associated Press accidentally posted his prepared obituary on the Internet, and when a member of the United States House of Representatives saw the notice, the Congressman announced his death on the House floor, complete with words of praise for his noble service to his country. It was only later that everyone in question learned that Hope was still alive and well in California.

Indeed, Hope remained in good health through his 100th birthday on May 29, 2003, and to celebrate, he was joined by a few other entertainers his age at a small celebration at his home. 35 states across the country declared it "Bob Hope Day", and Los Angeles named the intersection of Hollywood and Vine "Bob Hope Square."

Bob Hope died two months later in his Toluca Lake home in Los Angeles. A cut-up to the end, his last words were a joke. When Dolores, bending over his deathbed, asked him where he wanted to be buried, he replied, "Surprise me." Hope had converted to Roman Catholicism late in life and was given a Catholic funeral before being interned in the Bob Hope Memorial Garden at San Fernando Mission Cemetery in Los Angeles. Newspapers all over the world carried news of his death, with many running comics showing a grinning Bing Crosby welcoming him into heaven.

Bibliography

Crosby, Bing and Pete Martin. Call Me Lucky (2001)

Crosby, Gary and Ross Firestone. Going My Own Way (1983)

Crosby, Kathryn. My Life with Bing (1983)

Crosby, Kathryn. My Last Years With Bing (2002)

Faith, William Robert. *Bob Hope: A Life In Comedy* (2003)

Giddens, Gary. Bing Crosby: A Pocketful of Dreams-the Early Years, 1903-1940 (2009)

Grudens, Richard. *The Spirit of Bob Hope: One Hundred Years - One Million Laughs* (2001)

Grudens, Richard. Bing Crosby-Crooner of the Century (2002)

Hope, Bob and Carl Rose. *I Never Left Home* (1944)

       I Owe Russia $1200 (1963)

    and Pete Martin. *The Last Christmas Show* (1974)

Marx, Arthur. *The Secret Life of Bob Hope: An Unauthorized Biography* (1993)

Mills, Robert L. and Gary Owens. *THE LAUGH MAKERS: A Behind-the-Scenes Tribute to Bob Hope's Incredible Gag Writers* (2010)

Prigozy, Ruth and Walter Raubicheck. Going My Way: Bing Crosby and American Culture (2007)

Quirk, Lawrence J. *Bob Hope: The Road Well-Traveled* (2000)

Shepherd, Donald and Robert F. Slatzer. Bing Crosby: The Hollow Man (1983)

Strait, Raymond. *Bob Hope: A Tribute* (2002)

Made in the USA
Middletown, DE
05 December 2021

54342078R00036